Personal Finance for Women

Ricardo Moreno

Copyright Page

Publisher: Flamenco
Release Year 2025

Index

Female Power in Finance

It's long been said that finances are a man's issue. The images we see in movies, business magazines, or even on social media often show men in suits, making multi-million dollar decisions, and talking about investments as if it were part of their DNA. But this is just a poorly told story. The truth is, women have a natural power to manage money that is often underestimated or even ignored. And that power, properly harnessed, can completely transform your financial life, without needing a large salary or a silver spoon in your mouth.

Women have an innate ability to plan, organize, and think long-term. These three skills, although seemingly simple, are the pillars of good financial management. While many make impulsive decisions with money, women often pause, analyze, and look for a safer and more sustainable option. This doesn't mean they don't take risks, but they know when to take them and how to do so intelligently. This prudence, combined with their ability to adapt, is a winning formula.

Another great advantage women have is their ability to care for others. This may seem unrelated to finances, but it certainly is. Caring involves planning, anticipating, anticipating scenarios, and making responsible decisions. A mother, for example, learns to stretch her money, prioritize what's important, and find creative solutions when resources are limited. That ability to do a lot with a little is precisely what's needed to start building wealth from scratch.

Furthermore, women tend to be more disciplined with their goals. When a woman sets out to get out of debt, save, or invest, she does so with real commitment. She doesn't seek to impress or compete with anyone. She seeks peace of mind, security, and a better future for herself and those she loves. That deep motivation is what keeps her focused and steadfast, even when things get tough. In the financial world, that perseverance is worth more than any high income.

But there's something even more important: women have proven, time and time again, that they can achieve extraordinary things when they put their minds to it. They've done it at home, in business, in their children's education, in their careers. Why shouldn't they do it in their finances too? The problem isn't a lack of ability, but a lack of confidence. Many grew up with the idea that money was a man's thing, that talking about numbers wasn't elegant, or that they didn't need to learn about it if they had someone to take care of it. It's time to break all those beliefs.

Today, women have more tools than ever to take control of their personal finances. There are books, courses, communities, apps, support networks. Information is at their fingertips. And most importantly, they no longer need to ask permission to use it. They can and should be the protagonists of their own financial story. It doesn't matter if they've never saved before, if they have debt, or if they earn little. The important thing is to start. To start with what they have, from where they are, with the certainty that they can learn, grow, and prosper.

Creating wealth isn't just for those who work in the stock market or own their own business. Creating wealth is for everyone: for those who work in an office, for those who start a business from home, for those who raise their children full-time, for students, for retirees. Every woman, regardless of age, can make decisions that bring her closer to a more financially free life. And it's not just about accumulating money. It's about having options, living with fewer worries, being able to say "no" when something isn't right for her, and "yes" when something excites her.

Female power in finance is not a fad; it's a growing reality. Women are investing, starting new businesses, leading projects, managing households, generating income, and educating others. They are learning that their relationship with money doesn't have to be marked by fear or dependence. They are discovering that they can build something solid, stable, and lasting for themselves and for the generations to come.

Change doesn't happen overnight. But every decision counts. Every peso saved, every expense avoided, every wise investment is one step closer to freedom. And financial freedom is, at its core, freedom of life. The ability to choose, the ability to decide, the ability to live with peace of mind. That's what's at stake.

This book isn't intended to teach you how to become a millionaire overnight, nor does it promise you magic formulas. But it does want to remind you of something fundamental: you already have what you need to get started. You have intelligence, intuition, strength, and a motive. Everything else can be learned. You don't need to change who you are. You just need to start using that power that has always been within you. And once you do, there's no turning back. Because a financially empowered woman is a woman who never feels small again. She's a woman who knows that her worth doesn't depend on how much she earns, but on what she decides to do with what she has. And that, my friend, is true power.

Abundance Mentality

The way you think about money defines your financial reality, more than you think. This isn't just a nice phrase to motivate you. It's a proven truth: your mind acts as a filter, and what you believe determines what you allow into or out of your life. If you grew up hearing phrases like "money doesn't grow on trees," "money changes people," "better off being poor but honest," or "that's not for people like us," it's very likely that these ideas have been ingrained in your head as if they were laws. But they aren't. They are limiting beliefs, and as their name suggests, they limit you. They make you think about scarcity, lack, and fear. And that's the opposite of what you need to build wealth.

An abundance mindset is, simply put, the ability to see opportunities where others only see obstacles. It's believing there's enough for you, your loved ones, and others. It's letting go of the idea that if someone else is successful, that means you can't be successful. It's letting go of that idea of constant competition and starting to live with the confidence that you, too, can achieve what you want, even if you don't know exactly how today.

When you think about scarcity, you act out of fear. You make decisions based on "just in case," out of insecurity, out of urgency. You spend poorly because you think you won't have any more tomorrow. You settle for low-paying jobs because you think there's nothing better out there. You don't invest in yourself because you feel it would be an unnecessary luxury. You struggle to charge a fair price for your work because you doubt whether you're really worth it. All of this is the result of a mind that has been trained to survive, but not to thrive. And you weren't born just to survive.

The good news is that your mindset can be reprogrammed. It doesn't matter if you've been thinking a certain way for years. You can start making small changes today that, over time, will lead you to see the financial world through different eyes. The first step is to question what you've always believed. Where do your ideas about money come from? Who taught you what you know about saving, spending, or investing? What did you listen to as a child? Sometimes, just by asking yourself these questions, you begin to see things you didn't notice before.

The next step is to replace those beliefs with ones that empower you. You can start repeating new phrases to yourself: Money is a tool I use wisely. There are enough opportunities for everyone. I'm learning how to generate wealth. I have everything I need to prosper. At first, you may not fully believe this. That's normal. But your mind needs to hear something different to begin to change. It's like planting a seed. You don't see the tree the next day, but you know that if you keep watering it, it will grow one day.

It's also important to surround yourself with messages and people who reinforce this new way of thinking. If you spend your days hearing that life is difficult, that everything is expensive, that no one gets ahead, you'll absorb that as your truth. But if you surround yourself with women who are growing, who are learning, who share advice, who celebrate their achievements, you begin to see that there is another possible path. And that motivates you to keep walking.

An abundance mindset has nothing to do with ignoring problems or pretending everything is perfect. It's not about denying reality. It's about choosing how to respond to that reality. A woman with an abundance mindset doesn't give up in the face of difficulties. She faces them creatively. She looks for options. She asks for help. She learns something new. She knows that money comes and goes, but her value as a person doesn't depend on that. And precisely by being clear about her value, she becomes someone capable of attracting more.

Something very powerful you can start practicing is gratitude. It seems like a small thing, but it transforms your energy. Being grateful for what you have today, no matter how little, puts you on a different wavelength. You stop focusing on what you're missing and start seeing what you've already achieved. From there, building is much easier. Saying "I don't have enough for anything" isn't the same as saying "I'm organizing myself so my money goes further." Words matter, and what you tell yourself every day matters even more.

Another key practice is generosity. It may sound contradictory, but giving activates abundance. It doesn't mean giving away what you don't have or sacrificing yourself. It means sharing consciously. Perhaps you can help someone with your time, your knowledge, or a small action. When you give from a healthy place, your mind convinces you have enough to share. And if you have enough, it's because you're living in abundance. Even if you're still on the path to financial independence, you can act like someone who already believes in it.

Having an abundance mindset also involves making brave choices. Investing in yourself. Saying no to unnecessary expenses. Choosing what builds you up in the long run, rather than what gives you immediate pleasure. Sometimes that means getting a little uncomfortable, stepping out of your comfort zone, daring to try something new. But that discomfort is the gateway to growth. It's the price of leaving a small life behind to start creating a big life.

Finance with Purpose

Often, when we think about money, we do so out of urgency. We want more money to pay bills, get out of debt, treat ourselves, or simply stop worrying. But we rarely stop to ask ourselves why we really want more money. What's behind that desire? What kind of life are we trying to build? This is where the idea of purposeful finances comes in. It's not just about saving for the sake of saving or earning more for the sake of earning more. It's about using money as a tool to achieve a life that truly makes sense for you.

Money itself has no emotion. It's neither good nor bad. It doesn't make you happy or unhappy. What matters is what you do with it and how you use it to get closer to what you truly desire. Therefore, one of the most important exercises you can do on your financial journey is to sit down with yourself and ask yourself: What do I want money to do for me? Maybe you want the freedom to leave a job you don't enjoy. Maybe you dream of traveling, buying a house, helping your family, studying something new, or starting a business. Whatever your goal, you need to be clear about it. Because without a purpose, money slips away. It comes and goes, leaving no trace.

When you have a purpose, every financial decision becomes easier. It's not about cutting expenses out of spite, but about making them consciously. For example, if you know your goal is to save up to open your own coffee shop, it doesn't hurt so much to stop buying that daily coffee at the corner. Because you understand that you're giving up a small treat to achieve a much bigger dream. This is how you begin to build meaningful wealth: knowing that every peso has a direction, and that direction is yours to choose.

The problem is that many people live on autopilot. They work, collect, pay, spend, and repeat. They don't know where their money goes because they don't have a plan. They only react to the emergencies of the month. But you don't want to live that way. You want to take control, and to do so, you need to start by defining a map. Imagine your life as a journey. Money is the vehicle. But if you don't know where you want to go, any path seems valid. And that's very dangerous, because you end up spending without intention, saving without motivation, and making decisions that don't get you anywhere.

Therefore, I invite you to write down, with complete honesty, what kind of life you want to have in five, ten, or twenty years. Not just in terms of money, but in terms of well-being. Where would you like to live? What would an ideal day be like for you? Working in what? With what schedule? With what level of freedom? What things would give you peace of mind? What experiences would you like to give your children or yourself? This exercise isn't a fantasy. It's a compass. And once you have it, everything begins to become clearer.

From there, you can begin to align your financial decisions with that purpose. If your goal is to have more free time, maybe you need to build passive income. If your goal is to be more secure, maybe you need to save an emergency fund or pay off your debt. If your goal is to leave a legacy, maybe you need to learn about investing or financial education for your children. Each purpose has a different strategy. The important thing is to understand that money should work for you, not the other way around.

Plus, when your money has a purpose, it's easier to stay motivated. Because results aren't immediately visible. Saving is hard. Investing is scary. Starting a business requires effort. But if each step has a clear meaning, you keep going even when the road gets tough. Because you know you're not doing it out of obligation, but by choice. And that gives you strength.

It's also very helpful to divide your goals into categories. You can have a short-term goal, like saving for a vacation. A medium-term goal, like buying a car. And a long-term goal, like building a retirement fund. This way, you don't feel overwhelmed by the thought that everything needs to be accomplished now. You can move forward step by step, without losing sight of the most important thing: your purpose.

Another key thing is learning to say no. When you're not clear about your purpose, it's easy to get carried away by what others do or say. You spend on things you don't need, just to feel like you belong or to avoid embarrassment. But when you have a strong vision of what you want, you begin to protect your money more intelligently. Not out of fear, but out of commitment to yourself. Because you understand that saying no to something today means saying yes to something much better tomorrow.

Purposeful finances also mean that every peso that comes into your life has a mission. It doesn't just float away. It isn't spent thoughtlessly. It has a specific task: to help you live better, with more peace of mind, more freedom, and more meaning. And you can only achieve that when you're connected to what truly matters to you.

It doesn't matter how much you earn today. What matters is what you decide to do with it. Even with a modest income, you can begin to build a solid foundation if you have clarity and direction. And the most powerful thing of all is that, when you begin to act from purpose, opportunities open up. Because you're more attentive. Because you make better decisions. Because you invest your energy in what's truly worthwhile. And the money, little by little, begins to multiply.

So the next time you think about money, don't see it as a problem or a goal in itself. See it as a means. As a tool you can use intelligently, with love, and with direction. Ask yourself what you want it for. What kind of life you're trying to build. And let that answer be your guide. Because when money has a purpose, it becomes more powerful. And so do you.

Financial Diagnosis

Before improving your finances, you need to know exactly where you stand. Just as a doctor can't prescribe something without first giving you a checkup, you can't make sound financial decisions without first making an honest assessment of your current situation. Many people don't want to take this step because they're afraid or ashamed. But if you don't know the state of your finances, you'll continue to move forward blindly, making decisions that may take you further away from, rather than closer to, the financial freedom you desire. This chapter is an invitation to look at yourself head-on, without judgment, with the intention of understanding and improving.

The first thing you need to do is calculate how much money you actually earn each month. It's not just your salary, but all the income you have. Maybe you sell something on the side, teach classes, do extra work, receive family support, or have rent. All of that counts. Add up absolutely all your sources of income, even the seemingly small ones. Sometimes we think we don't earn enough, but in reality, we're not clear on how much is coming in.

Next comes the most revealing part: knowing how much you're spending. This is where many people are surprised. Ideally, you should write down all your expenses for an entire month. Every single one. From rent or mortgage, to coffee, transportation, gifts, grocery shopping, and "small expenses," which are those small daily outlays that seem harmless but add up at the end of the month. You can use a notebook, an Excel spreadsheet, an app, or simply your phone. The important thing is to be very specific.

Once you have that complete record, organize your expenses into categories. For example: housing, food, transportation, utilities, education, healthcare, entertainment, debt, and savings. This will allow you to see what percentage of your income you're allocating to each area. Many women discover they're spending more than they thought on things that aren't as important as priorities, and very little on things that would truly give them long-term peace of mind.

The next step is to calculate your monthly balance. It's very simple: subtract your expenses from your income. If the result is positive, it means you're living below your means, and that's good news. That surplus is money you could use to save, invest, or get out of debt. If the result is zero, you're right on the limit and need to adjust to avoid any imbalance. And if the result is negative, it means you're spending more than you earn, which is a warning sign you can't ignore.

Now, the diagnosis doesn't end there. You also need to review your debts. Make a complete list of what you owe. Include the name of the creditor, the total amount, the interest rate, the monthly payment, and the term. Debts often seem like a gigantic monster because they're all jumbled up in your mind. But by putting them on the table, you can begin to see them more objectively. Ask yourself which debt is the most urgent, which has the highest interest rate, which you could pay off the fastest. This clarity will help you design a plan to get out of debt without drowning.

Another key aspect of the assessment is your savings level. Ask yourself: How much money do I have saved? Do I have an emergency fund? In what account is that money? Is it easily accessible? An ideal emergency fund covers three to six months of your basic expenses. If you don't have one yet, don't blame yourself. Most people don't. But it's time to start building it, little by little, as a safety net for your peace of mind.

It's also time to review your financial habits. Are you an impulsive spender? Do you have a hard time saying no to certain purchases? Are you afraid to check your bank account? Do you often borrow money you never get back? Do you struggle to talk about money with your partner or family? These questions may be uncomfortable, but they're necessary. Your habits determine your results. And to change your results, you first need to change your habits.

A good financial assessment also includes reviewing whether you're generating income sustainably. Does your primary source of income depend solely on your time and effort? What would happen if you stopped working for a month? Do you have other sources of income that work without you being present all the time? These questions will open your eyes to the need to diversify your sources of income for greater stability.

Another important part is analyzing your emotional relationship with money. What do you feel when you think about money? Guilt, anxiety, anger, confusion? Often, financial blocks come more from the emotional than the mathematical. If you associate money with problems or trauma, you may be unwittingly sabotaging your own progress. Recognizing these emotions is the first step to healing them.

Once you've made your diagnosis, don't beat yourself up about what you find. It's not about blaming yourself, but about becoming aware. This process is like turning on the light in a messy room. You may not like what you see at first, but now you know where to start organizing. What was once confusing is now starting to take shape. And that, even if it seems small, is an act of power.

Repeat this assessment periodically. At least once every three months. Because your finances aren't static. They change, evolve, and require your constant attention. Over time, this habit becomes as natural as going to the doctor for a checkup or having your car serviced. It's part of taking care of your life.

In short, a financial assessment is the starting point. It's like looking at a map before embarking on a journey. You can't move forward if you don't know where you are. And now, after doing this exercise, you have something many people don't have: clarity. And clarity is power. From here, every decision you make will be more conscious, more informed, and more aligned with the life you want to build. Because you're no longer acting from confusion, but from understanding. And that changes everything.

Budgeting with a Female Perspective

Talking about a budget may sound boring, as if we're talking about spreadsheets, rules, and restrictions. But the truth is, budgeting isn't about limiting yourself, it's about freeing yourself. It's about taking control of your money so you can make better decisions, without living in fear that something will get out of hand. And when you approach it from a female perspective, things look different. Because women don't just manage numbers; we also manage emotions, family priorities, unexpected events, caregiving, personal goals, and a natural ability to see the bigger picture.

A budget with a female perspective understands that your expenses are not the same as those of the average man. It's not just a matter of paying bills. There are also expenses related to self-care, parenting, women's health, beauty, personal and professional development, the home, extended family, and often also helping others. Women tend to take care of not only their own finances, but also those of those around us. Therefore, a budget can't be a rigid formula. It has to be a flexible, living tool adapted to your reality.

The first step to creating a good budget is to be clear about how much money comes in each month. Whether you have a fixed salary, variable income, or a mix of both, it's essential to know your monthly average. If your income fluctuates, use an average from the last three or six months as a basis. And if you have high and low seasons, it's best to be conservative when calculating. It's better to underestimate your income than to overestimate it.

Next, make a list of all your expenses. And when I say all, I mean all: rent, electricity, water, food, transportation, school, healthcare, credit cards, entertainment, clothing, beauty, subscriptions, loans, pets, gifts, benefits, savings, and any other expense that's part of your life. There's no room for shame here. This isn't about judging yourself, but about understanding how your money moves. Only with that information can you make smart decisions.

Once you have your income and expenses on the table, it's time to organize them. You can use a notebook, an Excel spreadsheet, a mobile app, or whatever method you like best. The important thing is that you can clearly see where your money is going each month. And this is where the most powerful part of budgeting with a female perspective comes in: allocating money not just by category, but by real priorities.

It's not about following fixed rules like "save 10%, spend 30% on housing," but rather asking yourself: What's most important to me right now? Maybe you need to invest in your education. Or maybe you're saving to move, or want to start paying off your debt more aggressively. Whatever you prioritize is valid, but it must be reflected in your budget. It can't just be a wish in your mind; it has to be written in numbers.

A very useful approach is to use the percentage method tailored to your goals. For example, you could divide your income like this: 50% for fixed and necessary expenses, 20% for savings and investments, 20% for lifestyle, and 10% for personal development. But if you're at a point where you need to get out of debt, you can modify these percentages. Or if you're starting a business, you might want to put more money into your business. The important thing is that the budget fits you, not you fit the budget.

It's also essential to include frequent but not monthly expenses in your budget. Many women get thrown off balance when these unexpected expenses come up: their child's birthday, a car service, annual insurance, school supplies. But in reality, they're not so surprising. We know they're coming, we just don't plan for them. So, set aside a monthly amount for these annual or quarterly expenses. That way, they won't catch you off guard.

Don't forget to set aside a portion for yourself. Women tend to put their needs last. But that's not sustainable. If you're not well, nothing works. Include something for your well-being in your budget: an outing, a massage, a book, a therapy session, a class you enjoy. You don't need to spend a lot. You just need to give yourself permission to take care of yourself.

And if you have children, nephews, or dependents, use the budget as an educational tool. Involve them. Explain why you choose to spend on one thing and not another. This way, you're not only taking care of your finances, you're also instilling financial awareness in the next generation.

A great advantage women have is their ability to think long-term. We care about today, but also about the future. That's why your budget should include savings for emergencies, goals, and retirement. It doesn't matter if you can save a lot or a little. The important thing is to start. Ideally, saving should be automatic, like any other expense. Because if you leave it until the end of the month, you'll hardly ever achieve it.

Review your budget every month. It's not enough to do it once. Circumstances change: an extra income, an unexpected expense, a new goal. Your budget should be a living reflection of your reality. Take an hour a month to review it, adjust it, and celebrate your progress, no matter how small.

And finally, remember that a budget isn't a prison. It's a compass. It helps you make clearer decisions, avoid financial stress, and feel stronger, more organized, and freer. It's not about restricting yourself, but about directing your money toward what truly matters to you. And when that happens, money stops being a burden and becomes a powerful tool for building the life you dream of.

Smart Savings

Saving isn't about stashing away what you have leftovers; it's about deciding that some of your money has a greater purpose than immediate consumption. Many people think that saving is for those who earn a lot of money, but the truth is, saving is for those who know how to manage what they have. No matter how much you earn today, the important thing is that you start building the habit of saving wisely. Because saving isn't just a financial action; it's also a declaration of self-love. It's telling yourself: I matter, my future matters, and I'm going to prepare for whatever comes next.

Smart savings aren't achieved with occasional efforts, but with a consistent strategy. The first step is to understand that saving shouldn't be something you do only if you have money left at the end of the month. In fact, if you wait to see if you have any left over, you'll almost never save. Therefore, savings should be included in your budget as if it were just another bill. Just as you pay your electricity or phone bill, you should pay yourself. That amount goes directly into savings, no question about it.

How much should you save? It depends on your income, your expenses, and your goals. But as a starting point, try to save at least 10 percent of what you earn. If you can save more, great. If you can only save 5 percent now, that's fine too. The important thing is to do it consistently. Over time, this habit will create a cushion that will give you peace of mind and the freedom to make better decisions.

Now, not all savings are created equal. Smart savings differentiate between different types of savings. For example, there's emergency savings. This is essential. It's your safety net. It's the money that will give you peace of mind if you lose your job, if you have a health problem, if your car breaks down, or if there's an unexpected crisis. This fund should cover three to six months of your basic expenses. It's not money to be used lightly. It's only for real emergencies.

Then there's saving for goals. This is the money that will allow you to fulfill your dreams. It could be for a trip, a house, a new computer, a course, starting a business, or anything you truly desire. The important thing here is to set a concrete goal: how much you need, when you want it by, and how much you should save each month to achieve it. When you have a clear goal in mind, it's much easier to commit to saving.

You can also save for small unexpected expenses. Things like home repairs, gifts, family celebrations, unexpected school expenses. These aren't things that happen every month, but we know they do. If you don't plan for them, they throw you off balance. If you plan for them, you can deal with them without stress.

And don't forget to save for retirement. Even if you're young, it's important to start as soon as possible. Because time is your best ally when it comes to building long-term wealth. The sooner you start, the less you'll have to save later. There are private retirement plans, investment funds, and special accounts. Research the options in your country and start with what you can. It doesn't matter if it's small at first. What matters is the habit.

A common mistake is keeping your savings in the same account where you manage your daily expenses. This is dangerous because you can spend it without realizing it. Ideally, you should have a separate account, preferably one you don't use for anything else. This way, your savings grow without interruptions. You can also use automatic tools that transfer a portion of your money every time you get paid. That way, you don't have to think about it. It's done.

Another smart savings strategy is to take advantage of extra income. When you receive a bonus, a tax refund, an unexpected sale, or any additional income, save a significant portion of it. Since it's not money you expected, you don't need it for your regular expenses. You can use a simple rule: 50 percent for savings, 30 percent for leisure, and 20 percent for debt or investment. This way, you reward yourself, but you also build.

Saving also has an emotional component. Often, the problem isn't that you can't save, but that you don't want to because it causes anxiety. Maybe you're afraid that if you save, you won't have enough for other things. Or you feel like you're depriving yourself of enjoying the present. But saving isn't depriving yourself. It's giving yourself options. It's allowing yourself to choose calmly later. It's protecting yourself from difficult situations. It's empowering yourself.

And here comes a great advantage that many women have: the ability to think about long-term well-being. Women are carers. We care for people, projects, homes, ideas. And saving is also a form of caring. Caring for yourself, your family, your goals. Using that ability to your advantage makes you a powerful strategist.

Now, saving isn't the same as mindless hoarding. Smart saving has a purpose. It's not just putting money away just in case. It's saving with direction. With clarity. With vision. Knowing what you're saving for helps you stay focused, even when temptations arise. If you know you're saving to start your own business, to pay for your children's college tuition, or to have the freedom to choose your future, then every penny saved becomes a victory.

Finally, remember that saving isn't something you do to survive. It's something you do to thrive. It's a tool that allows you to say no when something isn't right for you, and yes when an opportunity arises. It's the step that separates those who depend on money from those who control it. It's what gives you the peace to sleep peacefully and the strength to make bold decisions.

So start today. With whatever you have. Even if it seems like little. Even if you feel like it's not worth it. What you're doing is much more than saving money. You're building a solid foundation upon which you can build the life you dream of. And that, woman, is the kind of wealth no number can measure.

Break with Emotional Debts

Emotional debts aren't found on a bank statement, but they often weigh more than bank debts. They're the decisions we make with our hearts on our sleeves and our minds off. They're purchases we make to please, to please, to avoid embarrassment, to avoid feeling guilty. They're loans we make even when we can't afford them, promises we keep even when they hurt, gifts we give to feel loved, commitments we accept so we won't be rejected. And all of this, even if we don't see it, has a real and profound financial cost.

Breaking emotional debt begins with identifying the place money occupies in your emotional life. Many women grew up with the idea that money is linked to love, acceptance, and validation. We were taught that saying no is selfish. That if we have something, we should share. That if someone asks us for help, and we can even begin to help, we are obligated to do so. And while generosity is beautiful, it can also become a trap if it becomes a way of constantly sacrificing ourselves to support others.

One of the most common mistakes is spending money to fill emotional voids. You feel lonely, you buy something. You feel sad, you go shopping. You feel insecure, you treat yourself to a luxury. But that doesn't solve the problem. It only covers it up for a few hours. Then the void returns, and the guilt of having spent on something unnecessary creeps in. It's a very damaging cycle: negative emotion, impulsive spending, momentary relief, remorse, and again, negative emotion. Breaking that pattern requires courage and awareness. Before buying, ask yourself: Do I really need it, or do I just want to feel better? And if it's the latter, find an emotionally healthy way to address that need.

Another form of emotional debt is lending money when you can't afford it or when you know you won't get it back. Often, you do this because you don't want to seem stingy, because you don't want conflict, because you're embarrassed to say no. But this sacrificial help isn't noble; it's self-abandonment. And in the long run, it breeds resentment, discomfort, and guilt. If someone asks you for money and you can't lend it without affecting your finances, it's okay to say no. Helping isn't taking on other people's responsibilities. You can support in many ways: with time, with advice, with contacts, with ideas. But your financial stability shouldn't be an emotional bargaining chip.

There are also purchases made to look good. That expensive gift for a friend, that new dress for a wedding, that trip you couldn't afford but everyone else was going. We spend to belong, to not feel lesser, to not look out of place. But at what price? Every time you spend out of social pressure, you're giving away your power. And the irony is that people often don't even notice the effort you made. What's left is your credit card with more debt, or your account with nothing. Your peace of mind can't depend on the approval of others.

Many women also carry an invisible guilt when they start to have money. If you come from a family where there was scarcity, you probably feel like you don't deserve to have more than they do. Maybe you help everyone, even without being asked. Maybe you feel that if you progress and others don't, you're betraying your roots. But you didn't come to repeat the same story. You came to break cycles. And the best way to honor your family isn't by staying where they are, but by showing that you can get ahead and help them intelligently, without destroying yourself in the process.

Emotional debt also arises when you accept low-paying jobs for fear of missing out on opportunities, when you don't charge what you're worth for fear of being called ambitious, or when you don't ask for a raise because you don't want to inconvenience others. But the money you're not paid is time from your life that you gave away. It's energy, effort, talent that you gave without receiving what you deserve. And that's also a debt, except the creditor is you.

To break free from emotional debt, you need to start practicing self-love in your financial life. And that starts with putting yourself first. Not from a place of selfishness, but from a place of responsibility. Because when you're well, you can help others better. Because when you're stable, you can share generously, not with guilt. Saying no, setting boundaries, valuing your work, and protecting your resources isn't being harsh or cold. It's being clear. And clarity protects.

Make a list of the situations in which you feel like money is slipping through your fingers. Review your recent spending. Ask yourself: Did I do this for myself, or to please someone? Did I do it out of freedom or pressure? Did I do it out of love or fear? This self-assessment may be uncomfortable, but it's liberating. Because when you understand why you spend, you can begin to change it.

It's also very helpful to have prepared phrases for saying no. Practice them. Write them down. For example: "I can't help you now, but if I can later, I'll let you know." Or "I'd rather not lend money, but I can help you find another solution." Or "I'm taking care of my finances, so I can't join in this time." Having these phrases ready empowers you. It helps you respond firmly without guilt.

And if you're already carrying past emotional debts, it's time to forgive yourself. Maybe you lent and never got paid back. Maybe you overspent out of insecurity. Maybe you gave when you needed it. Don't judge yourself. You didn't know how to do better. But now you do. And you can start acting differently.

Financial freedom isn't just about having money; it's also about letting go of the guilt, fear, and ties that keep us from making clear decisions. Getting rid of emotional debt is an act of maturity, courage, and self-respect. It's telling yourself: I deserve to live with peace, order, and personal power. I deserve to use my money as a tool for growth, not as an emotional burden.

You don't owe anyone your peace of mind. You don't have to sacrifice yourself to be a good person. You can be generous without forgetting yourself. You can give from a place of abundance, not scarcity. You can help from a place of conscience, not guilt. Because when you stop carrying what doesn't belong to you, you become lighter, stronger, more yourself. And that is the true path to real and sustainable feminine wealth.

Invest Like a Woman

Investing can seem like a complicated and even intimidating field, especially if you've had no prior experience or if the financial world seems fraught with complex terms. But investing is a fundamental tool for growing your money and achieving the financial independence you deserve. And as a woman, you have special advantages you can use to invest smartly, safely, and effectively.

First, it's important to understand what investing is. It's not simply saving money, much less spending it. Investing means putting your money to work for you. It's making that money grow over time, through different options that offer higher returns than a simple savings account. The key is learning how to choose where and how to invest, to minimize risks and maximize returns.

A great advantage many women have when investing is our natural tendency to be patient and analytical. While some people are driven by emotion or impulse, women tend to research, read, and make more informed decisions. That patience is valuable when it comes to investing because most investments don't generate instant wealth. Real wealth is built with consistency and time, and knowing how to wait for results is a financial superpower.

Before you start investing, you need to define your goal. What do you want to invest for? It could be for your retirement, to buy a house, for your children's education, or to have a financial cushion that gives you freedom. Having a clear goal will help you choose the right investment and maintain discipline.

Not all investments are created equal, nor do they have the same level of risk. Some are safer but offer lower returns. Others have higher risks but also the potential for higher returns. As a woman, it's essential to understand your investor profile: are you conservative, moderate, or risky? This depends on your tolerance for losing money, your financial situation, and your time horizon. If you're just starting out, it's best to be conservative and learn as you go.

A simple and recommended way to start investing is with mutual funds or index funds. These funds pool the money of many people to buy a variety of assets, such as stocks and bonds. The advantage is that your money is diversified, which reduces risk. Additionally, these funds are typically managed by experts, allowing you to learn and grow without needing to be an expert from the start.

Another option you can explore is real estate investments, which many women use to generate passive income. Buying a rental property can be a stable source of income, and the property can increase in value over the long term. But remember that this requires a larger initial investment and ongoing management, so it's important to research the market thoroughly before taking the plunge.

Individual stocks are another option, but they require more knowledge and monitoring. This is where patience and research are key. Learn about the companies, their results, their history, and their growth potential. Don't be swayed by fads or advice from "experts" on social media. Invest in what you understand and trust.

Don't forget the importance of ongoing financial education. Invest time in reading books, taking courses, listening to podcasts, and following trusted experts. Information is power, and the more you know, the better decisions you'll make.

A practical recommendation for investing as a woman is to take advantage of automation. Many platforms allow you to set up automatic contributions to your investment each month. This helps you stay consistent and prevents you from spending that money on unnecessary expenses. Plus, over time, you'll invest more without even realizing it.

You can also use your support network to grow. Meet other women who invest, participate in groups or communities. Sharing experiences will give you motivation, confidence, and new ideas. Often, the fear of investing comes from not having anyone to consult with or from feeling alone along the way.

Remember that investing isn't a sprint, it's a marathon. Don't despair if you don't see results quickly. Sometimes the market has ups and downs, and that's normal. The key is to maintain your strategy and learn from each experience.

Finally, investing as a woman is also an act of empowerment. By taking control of your money and making it grow, you are building independence, security, and freedom. You are demonstrating that you can manage your future with intelligence and determination. And this benefits not only you, but also those you love and the society that needs strong, financially free women.

So start today. Don't wait until you have a lot of money to invest. Start with what you have, learn, grow, and see how little by little your money works for you. Investing as a woman is one of the best decisions you can make to transform your life and create the wealth you deserve.

The Magic of Compound Interest

Compound interest is one of the most powerful and magical tools in the financial world, and it's essential for any woman who wants to build wealth to understand it. At first glance, it may sound like a complicated term or something only financial experts understand, but the truth is that compound interest is a simple and accessible concept for everyone. It multiplies your money without much effort, just with patience and perseverance.

To put it simply, imagine you put a sum of money into an account or investment that pays interest. Interest is the extra money you earn from having your money there. Now, with simple interest, you only earn extra money on the initial amount you put in. But with compound interest, you earn interest not only on the initial amount, but also on the interest you've been accumulating. In other words, your earnings are added to the principal, and in the next period, you start earning interest on a larger amount. That's the key: money grows on money that already grew before.

A simple example can help make this clearer. Let's say you save 1,000 pesos and your investment earns you 5% annual interest. In the first year, you'll earn 50 pesos. If it were just simple interest, you'd earn another 50 pesos in the second year, and so on. But with compound interest, in the second year you'll earn 5% not only on the initial 1,000 pesos, but also on the 50 pesos you earned in the first year. So, in the second year you'll earn 52.50 pesos, and so the growth accelerates more and more. Over time, this difference becomes enormous.

What makes compound interest special is time. The sooner you start investing and saving with this strategy, the more benefits you'll enjoy. The magic of compound interest kicks in when you allow your money to grow over years, even decades. We often think that investing requires a lot of money, but the truth is that starting small and being consistent over the long term can result in large sums thanks to this effect.

Furthermore, compound interest doesn't just work with money you have in savings accounts; it also applies to many investments such as mutual funds, bonds, stocks, and even some debts, so it's vital to know how to manage it to your advantage, not against you. For example, if you have debts with compound interest, the amount you owe can grow quickly if you don't pay them on time. That's why it's so important to learn how to leverage it to build wealth and prevent it from trapping you in financial trouble.

To get the most out of compound interest, you must do two things: start early and be consistent. Every time you add money to your investment or savings, you increase the base on which the interest is calculated. That's why it's so valuable to have regular savings habits, even if they're small amounts. If you put away a small amount each month, that money adds up and earns more interest, and over time, the total sum may surprise you.

Another key aspect is patience. Compound interest isn't a shortcut to getting rich overnight. At first, the results may seem slow or insignificant, but don't be discouraged. As time goes on, growth becomes exponential, and the numbers begin to increase much faster. This is why people who start investing early have a huge advantage over those who start late.

It's also important to consider inflation, which is the general increase in prices over time and can reduce the purchasing power of your money. Therefore, it's not enough to simply keep money under your mattress or in an interest-free account. Compound interest can help your money grow at a rate that outpaces inflation, so it actually increases in value and doesn't lose purchasing power.

Harnessing the magic of compound interest requires discipline and financial education. Many women feel insecure or afraid to invest because they believe they don't have enough money or knowledge, but the reality is that with the right information and small steps, anyone can begin to benefit from this powerful principle.

A practical tip is to automate your savings or investments. This way, you're not left to your own devices every month, and the money accumulates without you even noticing. This also helps avoid the temptation to spend that money on things that aren't a priority. And remember, compound interest works best when you don't constantly withdraw your earnings. Let them continue to grow and add to your capital.

In short, compound interest is a tool that can completely transform your relationship with money. It's how small, consistent actions can turn into big results over time. It's a way to make your money work for you, multiplying and growing without you having to keep an eye on it every day.

Understanding and using compound interest is an essential step for any woman to take control of her financial future. It doesn't matter if you have little money now; what matters is getting started and staying the course. Time is your best ally, and patience is your best strategy. If you give it room to grow, compound interest can work its magic on your money and help you build the wealth you've always dreamed of.

Start with Purpose (and Profits)

Entrepreneurship isn't just about opening a business to make money. Entrepreneurship with purpose means building something that not only generates income for you, but also has a deep meaning for you. It means connecting your daily work with your values, what inspires you, and what you want to contribute to the world. And when that purpose aligns with a good financial strategy, the result is real, stable, and sustainable profits.

For many women, entrepreneurship represents a form of freedom. Freedom of schedules, of decisions, of growth. But beyond that external freedom, there is an even more powerful internal freedom: the freedom to do something you love, that makes sense to you, and that benefits others. Entrepreneurship with purpose is precisely that. It's asking yourself what problem you can solve, what need you can fill, and how you can improve the lives of others with your product or service. When you find an honest answer, you are faced with a unique opportunity to generate real value.

Starting a purposeful venture requires deep introspection. It's not just about thinking about what's trendy or what everyone else is doing. It's about looking inward and asking yourself what you're passionate about, what you're good at, and what problems you'd like to solve. Maybe you're a good cook and dream of a small café where you can offer healthy food. Or maybe you're passionate about design and could help other women build their professional image. Maybe you're a mother and you've identified an unmet need in children's products. The important thing is that this project makes sense to you, that it excites you, and that it drives you to keep going even when things get tough.

Because yes, entrepreneurship has its challenges. Not everything is rosy. There will be days when you feel tired, confused, or discouraged. But when your business has a clear purpose, that purpose becomes your driving force. It reminds you why you started, who you're helping, and what impact you're making. And that clarity is what keeps you going.

In addition to purpose, you need to focus on profits. Because no matter how beautiful your project is, if it's not profitable, it won't last. A business needs sufficient income to cover its expenses, reinvest in its growth, and, of course, pay you what you deserve. It's not about sacrificing yourself for purpose, but rather combining that purpose with an entrepreneurial mindset. Passion and strategy aren't mutually exclusive; they complement each other.

Therefore, it's essential to pay attention to the numbers from the very beginning. How much does it cost to offer your product or service? How much can you fairly charge? What expenses will you have each month? How many sales do you need to cover them and generate a profit? Making these calculations may seem complicated at first, but it's part of the game. You don't need to be an accountant; you just need clarity and organization. With a simple spreadsheet, you can begin to project your revenue, costs, and expected profits.

It's also important to understand your ideal customer. Who are you talking to? What does that person need? What do they value most? When you're clear about who you serve, you can create more powerful messages, more appropriate products, and more effective strategies. Knowing your customer helps you sell without pressure, connect emotionally, and build loyalty that will buy from you again and again.

Many women fall into the trap of selling below their value, for fear of not being bought. But entrepreneurship with purpose doesn't mean giving away your work. On the contrary, it means setting a fair price, because you know what you do has value, and because you deserve a fair reward. Don't be afraid to charge a fair price for your talent, your time, and your effort. Learning to set fair prices is a way to respect yourself and your business.

Visibility is also a key factor. Today, thanks to the internet, you have powerful tools to promote your business without spending a lot of money. Social media, websites, sales platforms, and digital marketing are all at your fingertips. You just need to learn to use them intelligently. Share your story, show the behind-the-scenes, and connect with your audience. People don't just buy products; they buy experiences, stories, and emotions. And you, as a purpose-driven female entrepreneur, have a lot to share.

Another important recommendation is to surround yourself with other female entrepreneurs. Build a support network. Talk to women on the same path, learn from their mistakes, and celebrate their successes. Entrepreneurship can be a lonely journey if you do it alone, but if you connect with other women who also believe in their ideas, the journey becomes easier, more motivating, and more enriching.

Finally, remember that purposeful entrepreneurship and generating profit are not opposite goals. They are two parts of the same equation. You can have a profitable business that is also a vehicle of transformation, both for you and those around you. You can make a living doing what you love, and do it well. You can add value, grow, and make money at the same time. You just need to believe in yourself, plan smart, and act boldly.

Entrepreneurship with purpose is one of the most beautiful paths to financial freedom. Not because it's easy, but because it's meaningful. And when you do something with meaning, work becomes passion, effort becomes growth, and profit becomes a true reward for the soul. That's the true power of a woman who undertakes with heart, strategy, and vision.

Don't Depend on Just One

One of the most important lessons on the path to financial freedom is learning not to rely on a single source of income. We live in a changing world, where nothing is completely secure, and having a single source of income is like walking a tightrope without a safety net. If something goes wrong, if that sole source disappears, you're left without a backup. Therefore, diversifying your income isn't a luxury; it's a necessity. Especially for women who want to build real and lasting financial independence.

For a long time, we were taught that the right thing to do was to have a good job, with a steady salary, and stay there for many years. But today's reality has shown that this isn't always possible. Companies close, jobs change, crises appear without warning. And if your entire income depends on a single boss, a single client, or a single business, your financial stability is at risk. On the other hand, if you have multiple sources of income, you can lose one without your world falling apart.

It's not about working longer hours or becoming a production machine. It's about using your creativity, skills, and resources to generate income in different ways. You may have a job, but you can also offer freelance services, give private lessons, sell products online, invest in a small business, or monetize a talent you previously viewed as a hobby. When you open your mind to other possibilities, you discover there are many ways to make money.

A powerful strategy is to start with your primary source of income, such as your current job, and use part of that income to invest in other options. For example, if you earn a monthly salary, you could use part of it to invest in a fund that generates income, or to purchase tools that allow you to offer a separate service. This way, little by little, your money starts working for you, and you're not just dependent on your physical effort.

The secret is to create sources of income that aren't directly tied to your time. Because if every peso you earn depends on the hours you work, you'll always be limited. There are only 24 hours in a day, and you can't work all the time. That's why it's so important to explore options like passive income. This is income that keeps coming in even when you're not actively working. Clear examples include investments, digital products, rentals, book or music royalties, and more.

Of course, it's not about quitting your job overnight. Nor is it about chasing a hundred ideas at once and not realizing any of them. The important thing is to move forward step by step. Choose a secondary idea, something you can do in your free time, that doesn't require a large initial investment and that has growth potential. Test, learn, and adjust. And when that new source of income starts generating real income, you can scale it or look for another one.

Many women have dormant talents that can be turned into sources of income. Perhaps you're a great cook and could sell something from home. Maybe you have good taste in decoration and could offer consulting. Or maybe you're good at writing and could create content for brands. Everything you know how to do can be transformed into value for others, and therefore, into income for you. You just have to look at your life through different eyes and trust in your abilities.

Plus, by having multiple sources of income, you gain more than just money: you gain security, freedom, and peace of mind. You no longer live in fear that if something goes wrong, you'll be left with nothing. You have options. You have room to maneuver. And that gives you power. It allows you to make decisions calmly, negotiate more forcefully, and even take risks you wouldn't have allowed yourself before.

A key point is to organize your finances well so that each source has a clear purpose. Don't mix all your income as if they were one. Assign tasks to each source of income. For example, your salary can cover your fixed expenses, your business can go into a savings fund, your investments can remain intact to grow. This structure gives you clarity and helps you keep each source of income functioning as it should.

Finally, remember that this isn't just a financial strategy; it's a lifestyle. It's deciding not to put all your eggs in one basket. That you won't depend on a single person, company, or project to live well. That your financial well-being can't be tied to something as fragile as a single source of income. Because you are worth more than that. Your dreams are worth more than that. And your security deserves a solid foundation, built on several pillars.

Don't rely on just one person. Not because it's wrong to trust, but because it's good to be prepared. Diversifying your income is a way to take care of yourself, your family, and your future. It's an act of self-love, maturity, and financial intelligence. And although it may seem difficult at first, over time it becomes one of the wisest decisions you can make. Because true economic power doesn't come from how much you earn in a place, but from how many doors you have open for money to flow in.

Earn More and Be Respected

Earning more money isn't just about having a bigger bank account. Earning more is also about valuing yourself, earning respect, and putting into practice all that you're capable of contributing. For a long time, many women have felt uncomfortable talking about money. Sometimes because we were taught it was in bad taste, sometimes because we were afraid of seeming ambitious, other times because we didn't want to upset anyone. But those days are over. Today is the time to talk about money freely, intelligently, and with authority. Because if you want to be respected, you also have to respect your financial worth.

Earning more is possible, but it doesn't happen by accident. It happens when you consciously set your mind to it and make strategic decisions. To begin with, you have to stop thinking that your value as a professional or entrepreneur depends only on how many hours you work. Your value lies in your experience, your knowledge, your creativity, your ability to solve problems. And that's not paid based on time; it's paid based on results. If you continue to earn little just because you're afraid of not being chosen or because people think you're "expensive," you're weakening your position. There's nothing wrong with wanting to earn well for what you do. In fact, it's right and necessary.

One of the first steps to earning more is to ask for more. It seems simple, but many women never do it. If you have a job, it's essential to review what your work is really worth in the market. Find out what people doing the same thing as you, with your level of experience, are earning. If you discover you're underpaid, build a strong case and confidently ask for a raise. Don't wait for your boss to figure it out on their own. Present your achievements, show how you contribute to the team, and explain why you deserve to earn more. And if there's no willingness to improve your conditions, seriously consider looking for a place where they value what you offer.

If you're an entrepreneur or a freelancer, setting the right prices is vital. Often, low prices don't attract more clients; on the contrary, they make your work seem less professional. The key is to clearly communicate the value of what you do. Tell us about your process, your preparation, and the concrete benefits your clients receive. Don't just sell what you do; sell the results you deliver. And when you charge what you deserve, something changes not only in your bank account but also in your self-esteem. You begin to see yourself in a different light, and that shows. People notice when a woman respects and values herself.

Earning more also means learning more. Don't stagnate. Invest in training, in new tools, in expanding your skills. The more you know, the more options you have. You can improve your performance, offer new services, or access better positions. And it's not about having a thousand degrees, but about constantly evolving. Today, there are courses, workshops, tutorials, and books available to everyone. If you really want to grow, the information is available. The important thing is to use it, apply it, and turn it into a real advantage.

Another way to increase your income is to collaborate with other women. Competition among ourselves is useless. What is useful is uniting talents, creating alliances, and sharing networks. Two women who support each other can go further than ten who criticize each other. And often, a strategic collaboration can open doors you never imagined. So seek out peers, mentors, and partners. Share what you know and receive what others know. Shared growth is faster and stronger.

And don't forget one key point: respect your limits, too. Earning more doesn't mean working yourself to exhaustion. It means working smarter, more focused, more strategically. Don't say yes to everything. Don't give away your time. Don't be available 24/7 just to look good. Set your conditions clearly, stand by your word, deliver what you promise, but also demand the same level of commitment from others. Respect isn't something you beg for; it's built through firm and consistent actions.

Furthermore, it's essential to change your internal dialogue. Stop telling yourself you can't, that you're not enough, that you don't know how. Start telling yourself that you're learning, that you're growing, that you have the right to prosper. Because it all starts with how you talk to yourself. A woman who speaks with power moves with power, and a woman who moves with power wins more. It's that clear.

Earning more isn't just a matter of money; it's a matter of identity. It's about recognizing your worth and building a life that lives up to that value. And when you command respect in the economic world, you're also teaching other women that they can do the same. You're paving the way, you're showing a new way of being in the world. And that, besides being powerful, is necessary.

So don't settle for less. Don't minimize your talent. Don't accept unfair conditions out of fear. Earning more and earning respect isn't an impossible dream; it's a decision that starts today. You just need courage, strategy, and commitment to yourself. Because when a woman decides she's going to earn what she deserves, everything around her begins to change. And that change is the beginning of a stronger, freer, and more fulfilling financial life.

Equality and Clarity

Talking about equality and clarity in personal finances isn't just a matter of fairness; it's a matter of intelligence. For years, many women have managed their finances based on intuition, sacrifice, or habit, but not on information or power. This chapter is an invitation to leave all that behind and take the reins with full awareness. Because when there is equality in the way we relate to money and clarity about what comes in and what goes out, life changes. You feel more secure, freer, and stronger.

Equality starts at home. And I'm not just referring to your partner or family, but to how you see yourself in relation to money. If you feel you don't know, that you can't, or that you depend on someone else to manage your finances, you're giving away a power that belongs to you. Women have the same capacity as anyone else to manage, decide, invest, negotiate, or generate wealth. It's not a matter of gender; it's a matter of practice and knowledge. But often, due to culture or fear, we've assumed a more passive role. And that has to change.

When we talk about equality, we also refer to financial relationships with others. Especially in couples, where money can sometimes become a tool of control, manipulation, or conflict. That's why it's so important to establish clear rules from the beginning. If you live with a partner, it doesn't matter who earns more. What matters is that both partners have a say, access, and responsibility for the money that comes in and out of the home. Hiding, controlling, or ignoring each other doesn't help. Speaking honestly does.

In a healthy relationship, money isn't a secret or a battlefield. It's a resource managed by mutual agreement. Each partner should be clear about how much they earn, how much they spend, what they invest in, and what goals they want to achieve together. This doesn't mean mixing everything or not having separate accounts. It means respect, transparency, and clear agreements. And that also applies if you're in a business partnership or if you share expenses with someone else. Where there's clarity, there's peace.

But clarity isn't just for others; it's for you first. Many women have no idea how much they spend each month, or on what, or how much they really need to live comfortably. Or they live with a constant feeling of scarcity without any data to back it up. Therefore, the first step to living with financial clarity is to lay all the numbers out on the table. You don't need to be an accountant. All you need is a notebook, a spreadsheet, or a simple app. The important thing is to record your income, your fixed expenses, your variable expenses, and your debts, if you have any. No judgment, no blame. Just real data.

At first, it can be a little scary to look at the raw numbers. But once you do, you feel lighter. Because you're no longer guessing, you're making informed decisions. And that clarity allows you to plan better, make smarter decisions, avoid costly mistakes, and, above all, gain peace of mind. Knowing exactly where you stand is the first step to knowing where you can go.

Equality is also reflected in how we distribute financial tasks. Many women shoulder the entire household financial responsibility, in addition to work, children, and personal responsibilities. Others, on the other hand, leave everything in the hands of their partner or a family member and remain completely uninvolved. Neither of these extremes is healthy. Balance lies in assuming your share of responsibility, without overburdening yourself or disconnecting. And, if there is another person with whom you share finances, ensure that person also participates actively and fairly.

A key aspect of achieving equality and clarity is knowing how to say no. Saying no when someone wants you to pay for something that isn't your responsibility. Saying no when a work relationship doesn't value your efforts. Saying no when someone asks you for a loan and you know you won't get it back. Saying no when a purchase looks nice but isn't in your budget. Having clarity also means having boundaries. Because when you know what you want to achieve, you don't let anything or anyone get in your way.

Furthermore, it's essential to have clear goals. It's not just about saving for the sake of saving or spending less. It's about knowing what you want to achieve with your money. Do you want to travel, invest, have an emergency fund, pay for your studies, buy a house, stop working for someone else? Every goal requires a strategy and a plan. But if you're not clear, money is spent on things that don't get you closer to your dreams. On the other hand, when you have well-defined goals, every financial decision makes sense.

And finally, remember that equality and clarity aren't a destination; they're a process. You'll have good days and bad days. Months of organization and months where everything seems out of control. That's okay. The important thing is to stay committed to yourself. To return to your numbers, to adjust what needs adjusting, to keep learning. Because a woman who manages her money clearly and lives from a place of equality becomes unstoppable.

There's nothing more powerful than looking at your account and knowing exactly what's in it. There's nothing more liberating than making decisions without asking permission. There's nothing more courageous than sitting in front of the mirror and saying: today I am the owner of my money and my life. Because when there's equality and clarity, everything else begins to fall into place. And then, your relationship with money stops being a source of worry and becomes a source of power, well-being, and freedom.

Finances in Motherhood

Having children completely transforms your life, and it also transforms the way you view money. Suddenly, your financial decisions no longer affect only you, but also the well-being of one or more people who depend on you in every way. Motherhood demands that you be stronger, more forward-thinking, more organized. And, although you sometimes feel overwhelmed, it's also an opportunity to become an even more powerful woman. Because when you manage your finances wisely during motherhood, you not only guarantee stability for your children, you also guarantee freedom for yourself.

One of the first things to say bluntly is that parenting is hard. From diapers to college, every stage of life has its financial challenges. That's why it's essential to have a plan, even if motherhood arrives unplanned. It's not about having everything figured out; it's about taking control step by step. The first step is to create a budget that reflects this new reality. Write down all the fixed expenses related to your son or daughter: food, healthcare, education, clothing, transportation, activities. Add up your personal and household expenses. Seeing everything together will give you a clearer idea of what you need to cover month by month.

The most common mistake is believing that being a mother means putting yourself off until later. Many women sacrifice their financial well-being, thinking it's the right thing to do for the sake of their children. And of course, your children are a priority, but not at the expense of your stability. When you put yourself last, you're setting a dangerous example. Your children also learn how to treat themselves through what they see in you. If you neglect yourself, if you stop growing, if you live in debt or stress, they'll notice. Therefore, continuing to take care of your personal finances isn't selfishness; it's responsibility.

Another key point at this stage is having an emergency fund. And it's non-negotiable. With children, anything can happen: the flu, an accident, an unexpected school need. Having an emergency fund gives you peace of mind to face those unexpected events without going into debt. Ideally, this fund should cover at least three months of your total expenses, including those of your child. If you don't have one right now, start by setting aside a small amount each month, even if it's just twenty or fifty pesos. The important thing is consistency.

If you're raising a child alone, more than ever, you need to be strategic with your money. No one else is going to fill that gap for you. Seek support, yes, but don't wait around. Start thinking about additional income. You can sell something, offer a service, or use your talents to generate extra income from home. Even if you're employed, it's always helpful to have a second source of income. Keep in mind that this can give you the necessary margin to save, invest, or simply breathe easier at the end of the month.

Motherhood is also a good time to review your insurance plans. Having adequate medical coverage, life insurance, or accident insurance can make a huge difference if something were to happen. You don't like to think about it, I understand, but not preparing is leaving your future and that of your children to chance. You don't have to pay a fortune, but you do have to have the basics covered. And if you find it difficult to choose or compare, ask someone who knows for help, but don't let it go.

Furthermore, it's never too early to think about your children's educational future. It doesn't matter if they're still in kindergarten. The earlier you start, the easier it will be. You can open a specific account for that purpose and deposit even a small amount each month. In the long run, this becomes a cushion that can help you pay for school, books, courses, or even a degree. And beyond money, you're teaching them from a young age the importance of preparing and thinking about tomorrow.

Don't let guilt eat you up. Many mothers feel guilty about working, about saving, about not being able to give as much as they'd like. But I assure you one thing: your children don't need luxuries; they need you—present, calm, and strong. A mother stressed by debt or without financial independence has fewer tools to raise children with freedom. On the other hand, a mother who takes care of her money is also setting an example of empowerment for her children. And that's worth more than any expensive toy.

If you're in a relationship, it's essential that both of you be involved in the family finances. Don't shoulder the entire burden alone. Talk about expenses, make decisions together, define who contributes what, and how you organize yourselves. If you stayed home to take care of the baby, that's also work, and it should be reflected in your financial management. It's not about arguing over every penny, but about creating a fair system. Often, a lack of clarity at this stage generates resentment that can be avoided with communication and agreements from the beginning.

And don't forget about yourself. Motherhood doesn't erase your dreams, your goals, or your right to grow. Keep studying if you want, pursue your own business if you can, and build your support network. Remember that being a mother doesn't diminish your professional value; on the contrary, it makes you more organized, more empathetic, and more decisive. And those are highly sought-after qualities in the world of work and business. So don't back down. Use motherhood as a driver, not a brake.

Having organized finances during motherhood doesn't mean having everything under control all the time. There will be months that are more difficult than others, unexpected expenses, and fatigue. But with a plan, a firm mindset, and a dose of patience, you'll be able to navigate each stage with greater stability and confidence. Because in the end, the best legacy you can leave your children isn't just your savings, but the example of a mother who knew how to take care of them without neglecting herself. A woman who managed her money wisely, who remained strong, and who never relinquished her power. And that, without a doubt, will stay with them for the rest of their lives.

Circle of Rich Women

One of the most powerful, yet sometimes underappreciated, truths is that the environment you live in has a direct impact on your wealth. Not just financially, but also on your mindset, your decisions, and your results. Therefore, if you want to build a strong and abundant financial life, one of the most important decisions you can make is to choose the people you surround yourself with wisely. In particular, to seek out and create what I call a circle of wealthy women. I'm not just talking about women with lots of money in the bank, but about women who think big, who value their growth, who take care of their finances, and who are willing to support one another in achieving financial freedom.

Surrounding yourself with women who have similar goals transforms you. It drives you. It forces you to raise your standards. If all your conversations revolve around scarcity, problems, rising prices, or closing opportunities, your mindset gets used to living in survival mode. But if you start spending time with women who talk about investments, business, smart savings, independence, and growth strategies, your mindset changes. You realize you're not alone, that others are also on this path, and that motivates you to move forward with greater clarity and strength.

The Wealthy Women's Circle is a space where community is built, not competition. In a culture that often taught us to compare ourselves, criticize one another, or compete for attention, creating such a circle is a revolutionary act. It tells the world: together we are stronger. And it's true. Sharing experiences, ideas, connections, mistakes, and successes with other women who also want to grow can save you years of frustration and give you access to opportunities you would never have discovered on your own.

The most interesting thing is that you don't need to know millionaire women to get started. You can form your circle with friends, colleagues, classmates, or even women you meet at events, on social media, or in courses. The important thing is that everyone is willing to learn, grow, and share without judgment. You can meet once a month, for example, to talk about financial goals, review your progress, study a topic of interest together, or simply support each other when someone is going through a difficult time. That collective energy is powerful and keeps you focused.

Often, women get used to being the problem solvers for everyone else except their own. In a circle of wealthy women, that pattern is broken. Here, each woman is responsible for her own path, but knows she has the support of others who understand what it means to strive, fall, and try again. It's a space of honesty, but also of shared ambition. There's no shame in wanting to earn more, invest better, or get out of debt. On the contrary, it's celebrated.

Furthermore, this type of community helps you break down many limiting beliefs you may be carrying around without realizing it. For example, the idea that talking about money is in bad taste, or that if you do well, others will feel uncomfortable, or that success has to come with extreme sacrifice. When you hear other women speak freely about these topics, you give yourself permission to do the same. And that liberates you.

Another concrete advantage is that such a circle opens doors for you. Perhaps one of the women knows of a job opportunity that suits you. Perhaps another wants to launch a project and needs a partner. Perhaps a third has already resolved something you're struggling with and can show you the way. Support networks aren't just emotional; they're also strategic. The stronger and more diverse your network is, the more likely you are to grow.

And if right now you feel like you don't have any women around you who think like this, don't worry. You can start alone and attract them. Join online groups, participate in workshops, write in forums, start following accounts that talk about finances for women, and join training sessions. When you align yourself with this energy of growth, you'll begin to meet other women who are on the same wavelength. Sometimes a simple conversation can be the beginning of a deep connection.

It's also important to nurture the group's energy. A circle of wealthy women isn't a club for complaining. It's a space for growth. It's okay to share difficulties, but always with the intention of finding solutions, not staying stuck. The rule is: we talk about problems, yes, but always looking for ways to solve them. We celebrate achievements, learn from mistakes, and push each other to do our best. It's not therapy, even if it sometimes feels like it. It's an alliance of women who take their financial power seriously.

Some women tell me they don't want to share their financial situation out of shame. And it's understandable. We've been taught to hide our mistakes, to pretend, to not talk about money as if it were something dirty. But the more we hide it, the harder it becomes to heal. That's why, in a healthy environment, there's no judgment. There's only room to move forward. And if you're afraid to expose yourself, you can start small. Share a goal, a doubt, an idea. You don't have to share everything, just take the first step.

Ultimately, what I want to convey to you is that the path to financial freedom doesn't have to be a lonely one. And it shouldn't be. Women, by nature, are social, collaborative, and intuitive. We have an enormous capacity to create strong networks. Let's use that power in finances as well. Forming a circle of wealthy women not only helps you grow financially, it also transforms you as a person. It gives you clarity, it gives you strength, and it reminds you that you are not alone. Because when a woman grows, we all grow with her. And if we walk together, there is no ceiling we cannot break.

Your Financial Legacy

Thinking about your financial legacy may seem distant, even unnecessary if you're still trying to get your finances in order or build your first savings fund. But I assure you, it's one of the most powerful and transformative decisions you can make. Because legacy isn't just about what you leave behind when you're gone, but about what you're building today so that your life has a lasting impact. Your financial legacy begins the moment you decide you're going to do something meaningful with your money. And I don't mean having millions, but rather understanding that every financial decision you make today is a seed that can grow and bear fruit for generations to come.

Many women grow up believing their role is only to care for, support, or survive. But a woman can also be a generator of wealth, a driver of change, a leader of a new story in her family. The financial legacy begins when you change that narrative and decide to write a new one. Perhaps you come from a family where talking about money was taboo, where there were always shortages, where no one taught you how to save, invest, or plan for the future. And yet, you can be the turning point. You can be the woman who transforms history. And that is the true legacy: breaking cycles of scarcity to open paths to abundance.

Building a financial legacy involves many things, but it boils down to one clear idea: your money has a purpose beyond you. Every peso you save, every decision you make, every habit you adopt can be the foundation for a more stable life, not only for you, but for your children, your grandchildren, your nieces and nephews, even your community. If you think big, your influence can reach far beyond your immediate family. Because when a woman educates herself financially and begins to generate wealth, she inevitably inspires others to do the same. And that chain of inspiration is part of your legacy.

One of the most direct ways to build a legacy is through financial education. If you have daughters or sons, teach them from a young age about the value of money, how to manage it, how to save, and how to make smart decisions. It's not about giving them a fortune, but about giving them tools. If your children grow up knowing that money isn't a shameful or complicated topic, that they can use it as a tool to live with freedom and purpose, you are already leaving an immense gift. The knowledge you give them today can save them from many mistakes and give them the confidence to take control of their lives.

Another pillar of legacy is planning. Many people avoid talking about wills, insurance, emergency funds, or long-term investments because they think those are for the wealthy. But that's not the case. You don't need much to plan wisely. A clear will, for example, can save your family from many legal and emotional problems. Well-chosen life insurance can be the difference between leaving a burden or an opportunity. Thinking about your retirement today, even if you're far from that stage, is a way to respect yourself and those around you. Because when a woman takes care of herself, she also takes care of her loved ones.

The legacy is also in your everyday decisions. In the example you set when you choose not to go into unnecessary debt, when you choose to buy consciously, when you start a business, when you invest, when you talk to other women about money without guilt or fear. Each of these actions has an impact. And that impact multiplies. If your niece sees you reading a financial book, if your friend listens to you talk about how you organized your budget, if your children see you saving for a goal, you are sowing. You may not see all the fruits, but that is precisely the legacy: leaving something that grows even when you are no longer here to see it.

A very powerful part of financial legacy is also deciding which causes you want to support. Perhaps you want to donate a portion of your income to a foundation, support local entrepreneurs, or create a fund to help women in difficult situations. The scale doesn't matter; the intention does. When your money starts to have a positive impact on the lives of others, it becomes something much bigger than numbers in an account. It becomes a tool for transformation.

And you don't have to wait until you're older to think about this. Your legacy is built now, with the decisions you make every day. By learning about finances, getting your accounts in order, setting goals, and talking about money naturally, you're creating a solid foundation. It doesn't matter if you start from scratch. The important thing is to begin. Because every step counts. Every advance, no matter how small, is part of the history you're going to leave behind.

I also want you to know that your financial legacy doesn't have to look like anyone else's. It doesn't have to be spectacular or magazine-worthy. It can be quiet, steady, and deeply meaningful. It can be raising financially literate children, it can be paying off your house and leaving it debt-free, it can be achieving independence and showing others that they can do it too. Your legacy is yours. It's your mark on the world.

In short, thinking about your financial legacy isn't a matter of age or wealth. It's a conscious decision. It's understanding that your financial decisions have power, that they can improve your life and the lives of others, that they can change entire stories. And the most beautiful thing is that it's in your hands. You have the ability to choose what story you want to leave behind. And if you're reading this, it's because you've already begun to build one. May it be strong, free, generous, and deeply yours. That is the most powerful mark you can leave.

www.ingramcontent.com/pod-product-compliance
Lightning Source LLC
LaVergne TN
LVHW090421210926
848480LV00002B/639
* 9 7 9 8 2 3 1 1 3 1 6 2 4 *

PREFACE

The subject of barbed wire and its applications to some people is often taken for granted or holds little or no significance at all. To the rancher or farmer it is a basic tool to the infrastructure of their enterprise. Yet to others it becomes a hobby for collectors.

Barbed wire is perhaps one of the most significant products ever invented. It evolved through some dramatic changing times and survived to where it became the most sought after fencing material to date.

Fortunes were made and lost during the peak of the invention period. Lawsuits for patent infringement ran rampant in the 1860's through 1890's.

History acknowledges the pioneer inventors of barbed wire such as Joseph Farwell Glidden, Jacob Haish, Isaac L. Ellwood, T.V. Allis, George C. Baker, Jacob Brinkerhoff, Thomas H. Dodge, E.M. Crandal, Michael Kelly, Hiram B. Scutt, John Stubbe, Charles Francis Washburn and many, many others.

Hundreds and hundreds of wire types, styles, and variations were patented and manufactured to meet the ever changing needs of an expanding West.

For a more comprehensive explanation into the history of barbed wire and the people behind the inventions and manufacturing plants, the reader should reference the publications listed in the bibliography section for a more in depth study.

Barbed wire is rich in history and intrigue, a collector's dream. Wire collecting throughout North America and around the world is steadily on the rise. Wire enthusiasts are busy everywhere promoting the principals of:

"Preserving Historical Artifacts for the Welfare of a Time yet to be"

MERRILL'S FOUR POINT
L&J MERRILL 1871

ACKNOWLEDGEMENTS

History reminds us of events that have past. They are recorded for our reference and wise use, hopefully for the general good of all. The need for reference materials and the assistance of others became abundantly clear to me, early on in this project. Without this help and the encouragement of fellow barbed wire collectors, family, friends and acquaintances this particular story and collectors reference guide would likely not have been published. I sincerely hope that all reference materials listed in the Bibliography Section have been correctly and fairly used and that the burden of wise use has been met. This invaluable material is very much appreciated.

My thanks to people like Delbert Trew, curator of the Devil's Rope museum in McLean, Texas, and editor of "The Barbed Wire Collector" magazine; John Mantz ("Barbed Wire John"), founder and editor of the American Barbed Wire Collectors Association, Bakersfield, California; Dan Sowle, editor of the "Wire Barb and Nail" newsletter, Stanley, New Mexico; and a very special thanks to Robert and Julie Goss, of Goss Publishing, Kamloops, British Columbia, Canada for their tireless efforts, expertise and many hours spent towards the editing and publishing of this book.

To all of these people and the many others, thank you.

K.E. Perry

REYNOLDS NECKTIE
H. REYNOLDS 1878